House of Voices

Also by TM Collins

Poetry

My Poetry
The Poetic Totem
Yabby Creek
Along the Lip's Edge
The Crooked Floor
The Ruined Room
The Cold Stones of Feeling

Fiction

Until a Shrimp Learns to Whistle

T M Collins

House of Voices

For Cheryl

House of Voices
ISBN 978 1 76109 433 0
Copyright © text T M Collins 1998
Cover image: Max Vakhtbovych from Pexels

First published 1998 by Polonius Press

This edition published 2022 by
GINNINDERRA PRESS
PO Box 3461 Port Adelaide 5015
www.ginninderrapress.com.au

Contents

House of Voices	9
Dust	10
Bone Poles	11
Hospital Room After Death	12
Photographer	13
Through a Window	14
Footsteps	15
Through a Child's Eyes	16
Manhattan Hotel, South Brisbane	17
Children	18
Manchineel Tree	19
Asbestos	20
Café	21
Elephants	22
Just Out of Cairo	23
Open Casket	24
Symbol	25
Blocks At Play	26
The Harbour	27
Edward Kelly	28
Day Into Night	29
Convalescing	30
Unable	31
Pebble Worm	32
Travelling	33
Shoelaces	34
A Day To Paint	35
Hunger In Motion	36
Tied Together	37
Together	38

One By One, 1853	40
Writing	41
At the Chalkboard	42
Hospice	43
Andrei	44
Digging a Hole	45
Landscape In Operation	46
Zoo Life	47
Steam Train	48
Born To Fly	49
Fish of Joy Lap the Waters of Sight	50
Tripwires	51
Suicide	52
Toki Bird	54
His Life	55
Ardentallen Street	56
Cupboard Love	57
Ultimate Male Mirror	58
The Diamond Necklace On a Girl I Met	59
Social Parasite	60
Handshake	61
Ke-Ree	62
Ambergris	63
41 Whistler Street	64
Acknowledgements	65

The world! – it is a wilderness,
Where tears are hung on every tree.
                    Thomas Hood, 'Ode to Melancholy'

House of Voices

'I would welcome a public inquiry – the deeper they dig the more good they will find.' – Joern Utzon, designer of the Sydney Opera House, March 1966

Unlike other kids you sat
by banks of strobing water
setting coasters of shale
atop each other.
Your thoughts treadmilling
about Mayan temples.

You designed the House of Voices,
only to have it altered
by the gatekeeper.

My first memory of the House of Voices,
when Dad and I climbed slow monkey like
the three-metre fence. For years its
nude form lingered in my head.
Now when I think of the House of Voices
I think of Joern Utzon, nothing else.

Dust*

Like dry ice on the window,
each print, each tiny part,

glued to the surface like minute
sweat pimples on a horse's nape.

Taking my handkerchief, I smear it free
from the cemetery on glass, leaving

a bluey tinge, a scarred record of time,
an imprint of dust, that smelt of life.

* on a partly-broken windowpane at Auschwitz, Poland

Bone Poles*

Wrapped awkwardly in paperbark,
placed in branches of a tree.

Forlorn months pass, the flesh
stenches away, rotting in darkness.

Taken ceremoniously from this palace
to rest stored in tomb of final peace.

White angular struts, bows, bone pieces
all pulverised to chalky soft powder

that is packed into decorated hollow
wooden poles, like miniature logs.

The sand of life, grains of bones, not
ashes, not dust, but powdered people at rest.

---

* Aboriginal burial poles are called Bardurru.

Hospital Room After Death

Entering, like walking in a minefield, I grip my heart.
The door swings as a tail, swap, swap, swap.
No raven perched above, instead a dusty wooden cross.
The window opposite, a huge glass eye, the walls
coarse flesh with stainless steel gills
near each corner, breathing quietly.
Plastic curtains hang lame, hiding teams of shadows.
A clock, lonely, time riding wearily on its arms.
Light crowds the room, polishes the chrome bed as a
delicate frail chair sits wooden,
cracked from the light's constant dry quips.
Heavy linen sheets, fresh covers of white canvas yap with
a starchiness, devoid of sweat and tears, devoid of life.
A cabinet the colour of tinfoil supports
an upturned glass that cocoons stale air.
As a vase waits, a yellow stain climbs its interior
and it listens to the floor crying for nourishment,
a diet of wax and antiseptic.
The room wrapped in a spool of silence.

Photographer

Archipelagoes of curves,
her body is brutal beauty,
eyes nibbling at her looks,

light bulbs huff, time is fickle,
it goes and comes as the lens explores,
surveys like the tide rushing, covering.

The camera is regimental, so are the waves.
She is a dream amidst the skirmishing of time
receding, and only the photographer holds the tide.

Through a Window

A rainbow cast on carpet by the
window glass, sun flakes
parachuting past leaves,

my vision is drawn to watch the
wind knocking air, rickety air,
as tornadoes of foam burst across

the sky's sheen and trees' shadows
deftly sidle over ground, the
barrelling clouds squeeze like a sponge,

a vertical quilt of rain, then heavier,
falling crystal seeds leaving
a light stubble on the window face.

Footsteps

Footsteps alone in the house, whispering floors and the
fish tread water, their mouths shuttering open-closed,

in tune with my heart as a whisker of light unravels
through the black glass of night, it hair-floats to

the floor, sweeping away sounds and I stand still, the
beat of my heart, the fish O-ing, visible echoes as the

light thread skittles across venetian blind like gills,
gills slowly pumping, resembling a naked shingled pulse

and as I walk, my heart beat becomes my foot beat.

Through a Child's Eyes

Figures frozen, heads bowed, a child's tan shoes
scuff soil like a delicate rake, back and forth.

The last hitch of blue nylon strap whips from the
cavity, snakes itself along the soil to lie at its

handlers' feet, as the pale wrinkled face of the garbed
man begins to twist and flex from torn words, words

tattered like the book they're read from, you'd think
he'd know his lines by now, forever acting out his faith.

His hands cut a cross in the air and his words disappear
like a silk scarf in a magician's top hat. But where are

the doves? The cars look uneasy waiting in line as the
child toe taps a rock, it skims the dirt and falls,

hitting the nameplate with a twink twink sound, it was as if the
nameplate was magnetised, drawing the memento from the youngster.

The child walks to the edge, turns, arms outstretched like callipers,
beckoning to a circle of faces as crystal seeds trickle down cheeks.

Manhattan Hotel, South Brisbane

Towering to coal-coloured sky a cream brick wall
with a capping of grey bricks, fine gutters
embracing sculptures of broken glass.

The moon hanging on its black noose reflects
silk light across the wall expanse, a chiffon
curtain conversing with the wind.

The glass tipped wall to shovel a man's kneecaps,
no sexism here, what woman would climb such
a wall to shear hands to red lace.

The shine of the sharpened fence stung my eyes
like needles in my tongue and continued chiselling
strings of light, pearls in the night sky.

Children

for Zachary and Spencer

Rabbit about, colouring the yard with vibrancy,
their faces igniting laughter, and for me, taking

away sad vestments of existence – adult dreams, and
the hose, aching rings of flex coiling in misery from

inactivity, and as the house strangles itself behind me,
they rabbit on under the winter canopy, knitted sunlight.

Manchineel Tree

The Greeks called you 'Hippomane',
meaning 'causing horses to run mad.'

Ground carpeted by your acrid bitter fruits,
the caustic pearly sap lying in silky puddles.

Your patterned white brown wood, cherished
in fine furniture…

The axeman wading through grass, the axe
like an attachment, an artificial limb.

The axeman lights a fire at your base,
to heat your trunk, warm your insides.

The axe blade dives, a thin wave of steel
ignites your flesh, the axe lilts as little

cleats of flesh are thrust out, as white blood
throbs thick on the bone smooth axe handle.

Asbestos

My Dad gave me a slab of asbestos,
a gift from where he worked.

Like a rock from a quarry,
a shell from sand,
a bone from a heap,
a branch from a tree,
a piece of rare wood
from the craftsman's bench.

I kept this bit of grey,
fumbled it regularly,
and then found out Dad
was dying from exposure
to this fibrous thing.

I still keep it
in memory of Dad.

Café

A weathered stone face greets you as
vibrating shadows of light make window

frames resemble shrugging shoulders.
Sheets of lace paper sandal brooding

chocolate cakes while little coloured sweets
sit on pillows of coconut. This is opulence.

From frescoed walls to the expensive purring
of the coffee machine, the wine glasses wink,

and candles sit as lonely lighthouses, flames
in eccentric movement in the manufactured air,

flames sliced at by gilt edged fans, as pink table
cloths float up from carved parcels of wood, slowly.

Elephants

We must respect, admire your death ethics, burying your

dead together like a family reunion,
positioned in plots, legendary graveyards.

Frightening, and bewildering are the attempts
to revive the dying, and when hope of recovery lost,

you encircle your relative, bowing your heads in mourning.

Just Out of Cairo

Sky melting from clouds' wings,
the sound of distant propellers

humps the air, diesel-like stains
floating yet the scenery is bulging,

palm trees smear the horizon,
sand like perfume filters in the air

and it multiplies, but of course there
is no music here, just sinking pyramids

like Venice gripping fathoms of water,
what a place to exhibit inhibitions of Nature,

or is She somewhere else. Beautiful date palms.
There is a lid of heat haze siphoning through

palm fronds, sunken treasures and I sight a
toothpick on the ground, supported by hundreds

of granules of sand, it spoils the scenery,
so far from home and I'm reminded.

Open Casket

for John Andrew Tate

Arriving on a perfect winter's day
the horizon at the end of the street,
entering the church, my feet like cloven weights.

The absence of body, a lullaby of breathing.
Banana coloured light plunged through dusty glass.
Reading from the scriptures the congregation's
faces resembled a multicoloured lattice.

Then I imagined you stooped in the church courtyard
twisting back and forth, hiding from view, acting
as if you were the Phantom, laughing and joking.

Now the indiscriminate memories, the crack of thoughts,
the tintinnabulation of your smile, the coaxing of
your humour and your face stroked peacefully with a
downward smile, so wry and haunting in its perfection.

Symbol

for Amnesty International

Hardened barbed wire fences
a lone silk candle.
Barbs pricking soft flesh,
cream scurrying down cell walls.
Cream, faded blood, faded by time.
I sit like meat in aspic or a child
in a Wendy house, not wanting to leave,
drawn by the flame's blinking eyes,
bleary from sweat of torture.
Hot molten flesh issues over the rim,
leaving a collar of life.
The watery eyes float in the
funnel of flame, flesh piles up below.
Sapphire centre of heat strobing
at my thoughts. Extinguish the fire,
snip the metal thorned bracelet,
flood the scene with echo of hope.
The flame sniggers. I hear
the hissing of the burning cord,
thousands of sighs locked in darkness.

Blocks At Play

for the lost children of Romania

'Take a child by the hand
To lead him into the future land
Give him a confident stride.

To treat a child like a king
Hold him with pride
Close to your side.'

– from the film *Betty Blue 37½ Degrees in the Morning*, by Jean Jacques Beineix

Break us up, take us apart,
stack us, it is your task.
Unmask us and ask us our names.
There is is an anatomy of freedom
not lost in heavy-handed reason.
An eye for an eye does not sit
well with plasticine and chalk.
Who will put us together again,
blocks of the future, so fine.
Not quite yet attuned to modern time,
put us back together, let us back to play.
We are blocks at play, young children.

The Harbour

Bradleys Head, Sydney

Summer's early morning waterscape painting trickles down
from a line in the sky where night's blind is held tight.

The sun released like golden beans from a tin can, then
gradually yachts roast on the expansive blue hot plate,

sizzling shapes, bright poles of plastic yipp from side to
side, loiter at a point in the water as if held by a hand,

then majestically slither off, some zigzagging like a
stretch of cotton from a sewing machine. In the background

buildings crinkle, winking thousands of eyes as off in the
corner of the painting the white linen-like hats sit in

perfection, leaning against the blue wall. Minutes later.
Looking back, the sun has opened its gush of light – now the

House of Voices resembles egg whites stretched to a satin finish.
Ferry boats snail by and a hydrofoil wood-planes the water as a

pigeon heel-brakes to land on the rivered wood park railing.
The pigeon claw steps, then its beak begins tinking my wedding ring.

Edward Kelly

25 years of life, raised hell from
Kilmore to Kyneton, Benalla to Beechworth.
Poor old Jimmy Quinn was caught out.
Three fell Stringybark Creek.
Smell of gunpowder charged the air.
Judge Red Barry said hang
for Tommie Lonigan's death.

Maggie and Kate wept
like good sisters.

Then came the death mask.
Not many footsteps,
only their sound.
A rope squeaked on dry wood.
Dead weight and someone said
Kelly was real not like Robin Hood.

Day Into Night

Carbon fibres of morning,
fibres of a metallic sheen
inching across the work bench

of day as grass dew winks at the
collapsing backwards of the black
starred blanket into the rotisserie

of morning. Then, like fighter planes
peeling off, birds in formation, sink the
horizon pointing wing and dive sideways to

scribble the air with downward movement, this
is beauty at its utmost, flames of the sky enrage
their silver bodies, quickly transforming them into

the definition of design and as they become specks of
thought, far out of sight, the monster of morning bellows
more flames and the whole scene falls from the easel onto the

carpet of day, little pieces everywhere, a tapestry of colour, of
purpose, twelve hours hunching over in delight, until triste calls of
evening trisect the heavens and wait coldly for the touchdown of night.

Convalescing

With no gait, confined to a chair
like a canister on a dusty shelf.

Her body jitters like a Christmas
beetle on its back on hot concrete.

Clad in clothes, her frame bulges, a
scarecrow stuffed with straw, shoulders

resembling a straining coat hanger.
Tattoos, bluish nondescript symbols

adorn her porcelain white flesh,
delicate wrists bordered by blue

tie marks, imposed decorations.
Her flesh as cold as plasticine,

her eyes indigo that will never fade
emit a lazy glance, a horse's stare.

Unable

Blank hospital colours vibrated loudly, breaking the haze of
silence of this gruesomely austere place, a typewriter at the

nurse's station punched my temples, the sound somehow mimicking
the final aquatic cries, causing strange thrusts of thoughts,

irksome anxiety knotted inside my gut, the hurt like dirt, so much,
and I remember him plummeting down to be incinerated in watery space,

then his body twirling, coiling to the surface like a dolphin
levitating mercurially, the body sauntered on the water and with an

acrobatic roll lowered slowly and again surfaced, gasping, choking,
then buried in water with just a pencil-thin stream of bubbles

pouring upwards, I sat in the chair, wheels edged to the concrete lip,
the only sound the cackling of water spanking the pool walls.

Pebble Worm*

Lying dead, a buckled
floating submarine.
Ears, nostrils placed high like
dual conning tower and periscope,
closing by valves as you dive.
Eyes continually being polished
by wrinkled metal shutters.
Those same eyes weep, like oil
from a hinge, as you devour.
Allured, enticed, your prey
is torn apart by torpedo teeth
bedded deep in your pointed snout.
As iron-like jaws clamp shut,
you dive deep, leaving a spasm in
the water, a moving crater.

---

* The Greeks called the crocodile Pebble Worm.
Crocodiles became a protected species in Australia on 30/6/71.

Travelling

They drive, bellies scraping air,
their thoughts pregnant with hope.
If sex was the sole feeling
then it is now that the climax
is the joining of their existence.

He taps the steering wheel,
she checks the seat belt.
It's all in the movement.

They drive, bellies all alight,
thoughts flashing in radio delight.
The dashboard groans in green light.
She sneezes, he sights the edge of the bonnet.
The wheels, pulses of feeling tearing at bitumen.
The car an effigy of pleasure.

Shoelaces

Beside a tank stand, morning
diffuses afternoon, head hung
pinned to my chest, my chin
recording each thump of my heart.
I gaze at my school shoes,
shoes without laces and
to think my first day at school.

Out they came, Mother and Aunt,
having taken those brown lines
of thought from his caricature
of a body as each family member
walked into that darkened room
saying goodbye to the stiffened body

and they, my mother and my aunt
each with a shoelace, shoelaces
warm with his personage, taken slowly
from his shoes, shoes that were on him,
they threaded each brown lace slowly
through eyelets as if to signify the
lacing of death throughout my life.

A Day To Paint

The ferry triggers itself in fibreglass waves,
waves designed by a young itinerant artist.

City buildings are but a smudge as splashes of
paint jump, cluttered on concrete, confetti-like.

Passengers like robots transport themselves around the paint.
It's raining in the painting as the artist twirls time in her

fingers as if it were a green stem, the brush eyelids the canvas,
talking colours as it moves and not far away an old man grips

a bottle of pain as if it's stitched into his palm, his fingers
skinned in grime resembling worn crampons and his eyes split

olives hanging loosely to the scaffolding of his face, his brown
trousers look like mud in the sky and it's raining in the painting.

Hunger In Motion

A spider legs up leaves,
the moon shouting light on
its every move.

Crippled night air limps
across the yard of dark green as
stars sit, iridescent mushrooms

in the blackened paddock, the grass
moans, each blade of eyes turning,
watching the spider.

Eight limbs straining like tennis
racquet strings, a body weighted
like a sinker in mud.

With no crocheted net, the spider
piggybacks a sleek brown machine.
A final stalk of green, a drawbridge

against the concrete wall and a
crack into which is inserted the
polished brown parcel of meat.

Tied Together

for John and Malcolm

A young boy crouches grasshopper like, the eyes of his brother
beckoning him. Tyre treads evenly worn on both wheels, worn

evenly like the workmen's hands, the dirt ingrained in the fine
lines in the rubber and the chair, although old, still has that

shiny metallic appearance, chrome holds its age well as if each
night it is buffed with Hope as polish. The young boy begins,

first the left, then the right. Every morning, every day for
the past ten years he's done this task – he learnt to tie his

brother's shoe laces before his own. Then the brotherly duty
is broken by the cold stony stare from his brother's eyes,

eyes set like weak coloured jewels in a statue's head and its only
those eyes that are alive, a dual pulse of vision in a Crimplene

body, yet each day those eyes say thank you and the younger brother
just nods, nods as he has done for all ten of his fourteen years.

Together

for Anastacia

Like a rainforest.
A romantic setting.
Little quiet sounds
and I, like water,
float on a tissue,
then fall suddenly
helplessly into you.
Your molten flesh
engulfing all and
I keep falling into
a rhythm of softness.
The jungle rainforest
is in motion like a
quaint old sewing machine.
I move to a plateau and
see your smile.
Then in a torment of pleasure
throw it at you.
You grab and grab.
Rain bursts from clutched clouds
sprinkling the forest clean.
But the dust and rain
mix in a sordid mass of filth.
I'm stuck in this mess.
You slowly stop grabbing, rest
and wipe the water from my brow.
Your mouth is a mild smile.
It is exactly then that the moment
gives remembrance.

At the other side of the forest
where it does not rain,
Hell's grit is caked thick
with leaves, not green but brown.
I come running through a
hollow log, wet and tired. Your shouts and screams
rolling after me, abuse.
Echoing on, then race ahead of me,
waiting at the entrance for me.
I go faster, your voice is louder,
more taut and armed.
The log tapers, I brake at
my heels, and try to pass.
Slowing, falling down,
pouncing on soft green grass.
A fresh smell, wet, warm, soft.
Sliding sliding slowly, everything
is so much smaller now.
You grab at me, wandering hands
in distress, gulps and more.
I feel pale, you are blue.
I'm floating in a prism while
you gurgle and gargle.
It's dark and quiet and the
rainforest seems gone and your face is
silent and my feelings mix in
a paste of love and hate.
I remove my strained hands from
your neck and look up. It is late.

One By One, 1853

Whale bone excitement.
Indeed they frolicked
in the cutting blue.

One by one inched forward
by their own footsteps,
thin ankles bearing weight.

Each figure jumping, many
pushed, like a slot machine handle,
the reward, a slick pleasure.

Human remains scattered on
rocks like pigeon droppings
and to think they lined up

each Aborigine, each figure making
a snake line dangling in a fall
to the tirelessly suffering ocean below.

Writing

I drain my thoughts from my fingers as
the wall clock plays its internal tennis,
a continual rally, slowing batteries' pulse.
Outside clouds steam south meeting
somewhere in the dragnet of a storm,
birds drown into the blue, their
matted wings gleam and marble claws

drip from the muscles of thin thighs.
Blotches of ink on paper, handwriting,
like coiling nets cast out to sea,
my prey is a poem hurdling the view.
Staring eyes alter window from square
to oblong to panorama and sounds
mix with my silent breath like

fine sand washing in with the tide.
Like a cabin porthole thrust open
the weight of the view heaves and heels
my thoughts, I write, I'm powerless
in this confession between the chalk
and the blackboard, I write, my thoughts
like fish as the nets on paper, catch.

At the Chalkboard

It is essential not to have faith in human nature. Such faith is a recent heresy and a very disastrous one.'– Professor Herbert Butterfield, *Christianity and History*

I stood at the chalkboard
scratching away, I'd seen
Mickey Mouse hit Minnie just yesterday.

The priest stood up there
cajoling the crowd, a throng
all collared by religion.

And most all stuck and wallowing
in their little crimes
and lack of confessions.

Then in unison they all
stood and shouted each sin and
the priest heard each confession.

I saw Mickey Mouse hit Minnie and
I stand at the chalkboard, thinking.
But today I might just as well forget.

Hospice

for Ray

Teeth marks in the soap, flotation tanks
instead of blue-tiled swimming pools,

steel rooms, padded canister chairs and
stainless steel dishes, definitely no china,

fragility is an illness in this place of plastic
curtains that are stapled, the sniggering sun

singed a crease into a split, making a peep hole.
No books, no visitors, rubber pencils and paper

are therapy, attempt writing without injury.
At each dormitory door bundles of filthy linen,

the clean sheets help keep up the appearance.
This place reeks of human tragedy, reeks.

Andrei

A dissident, a prize winner.
Statue of stature in Gorky Park.
An example to all people and nations.
But the west unable to alter
the travesty of your existence.

You were confined to abject solitude.
Your benefits to the world
distorted and disputed.
A syringe administered by your
master keepers gave balance
to an already imbalanced life.

It was only a matter of time
before the scholar went missing.
Andrei Sakharov died an unkind death.

Digging a Hole

A bird treks blue ice, its wing beat, a whop whop sound,
the sound bothers me, somehow thumping my temples like

a drum in an empty auditorium, and flowers at the edge
of the pathway scream as a butterfly hangs in air like

a metallic and ceramic brooch pinned to a blue cardigan
while along the fence strands of tuber pinch past aged

palings, fingers wrapping around jail cell bars and on
the soil at my feet mustard-coloured seeds, ugly little

blotches like melanomas, then my shoe creases on an edge
of steel, vibrations of morse code transmit into my flesh.

Landscape In Operation

(Pepperina Hill, Lake Moogerah)

Water curled like butter, sculptured by blades of wind, mountains scraped into distant existence, as trees, fleshy reminders of life,

rattle green discs as the bark of earth buckles upwards in search of moisture, a wing-leafed bird punches the water, dips and dives,

submarines aqua depths, as other birds train in air leaving trails of afterthought. It is here, where time trips up. Another hits

the water, a fluid mushroom drawn upwards as the hooded cliff face poses behind a sheer wall of vapour, clouds garnish the line of blue,

a cable, a connecting line, the seam running left to right, journeying across the mountain's fringe, a dotted impression, tiny perforations.

If, with the wind as a knife, you pry open that line like separating teeth on a zipper to reveal the hidden mechanism of landscape.

Zoo Life

Strolling bitumen paths, peering over barriers.
Looking through bars at cages, blue rinsed concrete,
concrete pits and hot wired perimeter fences.
Nothing beats seeing wild animals up close.
Rare, exotic, endangered and primitive.

Saved from extinction for breeding, study
and research. So much easier in captivity.
Beauty and diversity of natural wild animals
not living relaxed in the natural world.
But in the zoo there is less stress,

animals are happier, so we are told.
Animals that pace, wander ceaselessly about,
eat their own vomit and faeces.
From jungles, forests and plains collectors haunt
and hunt limitless numbers, like skins or skulls.

The recreational dollar is powerful, collectors
scavenge on while more money builds simulated rainforests,
designed, created and cultivated to resemble nature.
Outside man cuts the mallee and levels the land.
Inside seals do drunks' tricks and chimpanzees have tea parties.

Animals in a tourniquet of gawk, novelty animals, freak shows.
And artificial insemination, embryo transfers, even contraception.
Supply the zoo, animals captive for public awareness,
entertainment, publicity and fanfares as the panda
gives birth to an offspring that will never see home.

Steam Train

On its round seats of metal the beast
whittles the lead like sticks,

off into the distance.
As night climbs the lattice of day,

it moves, a line of crows hunching
over the wire, following like carriages.

The blackened creature drawing the
darkness, off into the distance.

Born To Fly

for Wayne Blackmore, the world's first paraplegic hang glider

From grobian body you rose striving,
healing your wound into a spirit,
the dreams of youthful gods.
Dreams that are seldom harnessed
with respect by charlatans of thrill.

Twining yourself around the dome of sky,
traversing invisible dots, threads of air,
lines drawn by nature, whistling the feathers
of the wind, flitting in and out of bird's shadows,
often crossing swords with their pride.

But then on that July day the sun melted
the threads of invisible flight,
and once more you were plunged downwards.
With a grotesque flick of your wings
your flesh, metal and plastic cluttered the surface.

Trying to lever your body upwards into flight
you were stuck to the skin of the water,
your wings draped over the wound.
With one final lurch forward perhaps looking
for steps in the water, Wayne Blackmore was released.

Fish of Joy Lap the Waters of Sight

for Janice*

Your eyes ghostly lovers amidst the sand-papered darkness,
everything smothered in neatness, yet two faint pin pricks glow,
tiny bonfires in the dim recesses of lost sight, trickling
dreams into dashes, through time-carved dullness, giving hope.

Sounds truly tongueless, pewter sounds, always distant echoes,
other sounds nailed down to the scary dark wood-stained existence
resembling dusty antiques covered in grey sheets, blurred shades.
Dour and lonely your eyes as your hands became chauffeurs to sight.

Then an explosion of images, the double-barrelled blankness gone,
the smoking barrels empowered twenty-eight years of riddled thoughts,
your eyes simmering wasps held gaze in slow motion, then your sight
tiptoed the viewscape and suddenly the yap of a spinnaker was the

colour of the spinnaker and rain not a blousey sheet but little sacks
swinging peacefully as your eyes, wells of paraffin, were lit forever,
those dashes of dreams becoming the mango flesh of a November sun.
In removing the barnacles of darkness, you were drenched in sight.

---

* Janice, blind from birth, gained her sight at the age of twenty-eight.

Tripwires

An inordinate waste of shotgun
lead is making many more dead.

A blanket, a morose cover
of lead across our Top End.

Magpie geese pale and sick
from ingesting weed and lead

from the bottom of swamps.
Crocodiles, Eagles and Hawks

feed happily on heavy birds.
Man in pursuit of leisure

has set trip wires. Aborigines
love the flesh of these white

and black birds, it is tradition.
They too are dying of lead poisoning.

Suicide

for the poet Francis Adams

Someone clapped their hands as if introducing a scene…

Reading his poetry I uttered his prayer flags
and imagined him reading aloud with me,
a laboured breath chopping the air,
leaving torn echoes, memories from poet to poet.

He struggled with thoughts like Houdini with knots.
The chip hard to shoulder as death is hard to whitewash.
Grief scratched his sanity like fine sandpaper on silk.
The slavery of life, the edifice of death, made him write.

Wanton illness, strained youth, brought death snapping
at his heels, never retreating, devouring time's tablets,
one by one, ever so slowly devouring a lifelong dose.
Tears, not gentle waves on flesh but spitballs of fire on ice.

Like a moth on a pin, already an experiment on show.
In his mind no peace, no armour-plate against fate,
death was becoming magnetic, appealing.
It rode the pulses of thought in the corridors of his mind.

While death became a constant itch at the elbow,
the pen ice-skated paper, the blade becoming
worn and heavy in a dreaming hand, the other hand held
a sword giving secular balance to the pen.

His mind opened, allowing dust and air entrance.
The itch continued cowering along his arm.
More and more sheets of paper emptied space idle.
And the once-flamed ink began to cuddle in rest.

Perhaps, a pounding sudden death caught in a social
mousetrap on a crazed Saturday night in the turbulent
city lights, lights that strobe in tune with death's knell.
Should there be a code of death, a list of instructions?

Or, as in some religions, desire is linked with burning.
Burning carbonised thoughts, signals of a cinder nature.
But, as they burn, the heart beat is still the most
valuable musical note that can be heard. Which is best.

From the ambulance man to the tray of ash it's all grief.
Crowd the earth with skeletons like the crowded night sky.
One more is not going to matter, shout the laughing ghosts
as the diggers bend their backs in the ritual movement of dirt.

A corpse is a heavy object, nothing deserves to die, nothing.
But death was close, he could feel its warm snigger.
It had become his twin, practising life with him. Then,
Francis Adams raised a lump of iron to touch his head…

His wife sat nearby and clapped her hands.
Francis Adams was dead.

Toki Bird*

(Japan, 1992)

In an open clearing in forested mountains...

A bright red faced bird sits on a solitary perch in a
fully enclosed gilded cage with pocked padding inside,

it breathes by way of those pocks, porous spots and
the padding, there to save it from injuring itself.

It is the last remaining bird of its kind...

Waiting a solution.

* soon to be extinct

His Life

for the patient in room 4b, 9/8/87

The brazen bottle stood
empty of life.
His hand trembled at seeing
a hidden spider.
His nerves splintered,
senses all astray.
Tiredness was closing
like a nut on a bolt.
His thoughts like rusted
wrought iron, patches
of white paint,
glimmers of the past.
Holding the bottle as
if stitched into his palm,
I remembered the day we
drank to the success
of the operation.
He died a week later.
Pity we couldn't keep
his life in that bottle.

Ardentallen Street

Sitting in splendour
their oily coloured
coats glisten.
From tips of steeples
they move in cumbersome
flight shouting a diatribe.
Settling in Norfolk pines with
forceps feet and bristling feathers
at their throats, they look down
Ardentallen Street.

Cupboard Love

Your back knifes the bed in false anguish while
I think about the poem 'Don't Play With Razors',

the anger burns in your eye sockets, yet there is beauty
in those eyes as I wander the quilt for a cigarette

while you are limp and very restful, I've unloaded my
tensions, you've held them, contained them, my receptacle

and the smell of my sweat makes me guilty, the smell
of your rubbery flesh sickens me – I shove you from

the bed and lie, rearrange my body and sleep happy.
I'll put you back to dire cupboard darkness tomorrow.

Ultimate Male Mirror

A woman with
a masculine

edge to sex
that frightens me,

makes me vulnerable
and quenches

my free spirit.
The watery glass

cutting into my flesh
and leaving,

that silvery
finish of satisfaction.

The Diamond Necklace On a Girl I Met

From the region between right shoulder
and right breast, a breast heaving with

each sigh like chiffon curtains pulsing,
a shine of light, talking with each motion,

sparkling the air, talking mythology with
my eyes, mythology of woman, femininity,

shining little triangles, rectangles, cubes
of light, painting my eyes clear of all thought,

making the physical heavings of that breast,
below the soft shoulder, part of me, making

me feel the beauty, little lights caressing
my face, directly at me and her voice is an

echo tickling the walls, tickling the walls
as my eyes close, close in eyelid darkness.

Social Parasite

for Joseph Brodsky, fifth Poet Laureate of the USA

Branded 'Social Parasite' in your home land,
you were convicted like Andrei Sakharov.
Exiled to a work camp, left to leech away.
They hoped to suck any artistry from you, as
they had done with Mandelstam in '34.
Why do they persecute poets?

Under Leonard Brezhnev you were banished,
discarded like an operating theatre glove.
In Seventy Two you arrived in the 'Free States'.
You were awarded the Nobel Prize.
And now, you are awarded the post of
Poet Laureate in your home land.

Handshake

for Horatio Edward (Ted) Grose

A measure of respect, in your case, kindness and a heartiness,
a handshake that always meant a genuine warmth of greeting.
The grin, the smile, the laid back style, you at times reminded
me of a possum, sure of yourself but also unsure of yourself,

eyes like the possum's, deep in memory with warm magnetism, and
a hypnotic manner. You joked, you made entreaty of friendship, the
humanitarian, the persuader in a gentle way, with calm benevolence.

With your passing came initial thoughts the colour of pitchstone, with
some people when they are gone they are just that, you stayed in memory
much like the possum edging its way along the railing seeking company,
seeking quiet friendship, yet I remember most the distinct handshake.

Ke-Ree*

From a solution in whales' skulls
comes the cream-coloured suet.

Little precision forms it into
a slender tallow cylinder.
Embedded within from bottom to
outside top a fibrous spongy cord.

Down shaved smooth flanking scurry
veins of sodden cream silk, some
plunge as viscous droplets,
sitting idly in molten piles.
High above, the vindictive wisp of rope
burns in capricious delight.

White rope twisting about in
a sordid display of self torture
as melted grease issues from the rim.
The brittle stick thaws under
luminous intensity, wilting downwards.

The chord wavers and gentle signals
of smoke buffet away, as the pillar
of sculptured moon rock collapses,
leaving the Whale's garbled thoughts
splattered in mounds of wax.

---

* Ke-ree: the Greek word for candle. Spermaceti is a substance contained in the head cavity of the whale; it is used in the manufacture of candles.

Ambergris

Sent adrift carelessly by your maker,
your opaque ash coloured existence floats
calmly through tropical seas, being twirled
about by ocean currents, occasionally
being cast ashore to sit in peace.
You become prescription fodder to

hungry doyens of the marketing world.
Your worth, a balminess of aroma,
when heated your fragrance released,
hence your use in cooking finery.
That same musky smell the perpetrator
in the success stories of perfume makers.

It is left to mechanical knives aboard
bloodied ships of torture to wrench you
from the whale's belly.
No matter, to the whale you are
just a morbid secretion of cholesterol and
steroids, discarded into the sea.

41 Whistler Street

Every day in a cane chair
outside his front gate,
watching the traffic.

When he died she pressed
eighty-seven candles in
the lawn, lit them and

sat watching the slender
hands of chalky flame
quavering in prayer,

forming a net of yellowy
light, lustreless scales
on grass sealed his rest.

Acknowledgements

Thanks to Les Murray for his encouragement and special thanks to Nigel Krauth for his inspirational advice.

Poems in this collection have previously appeared in the following publications: *Australian Writers' Journal, Blast, Cargo, Coppertales, four W, Grassroots, Harvester, Heartland, Idiom 23, Imago, Mattoid, Metro Arts Review, The Muse, New Decade, Northern Perspective, Outrider, Public Poetry* (Brisbane Bus Poetry Posters), *Quadrant, Rocky Hill Lines, Scope, Social Alternatives, Southern Review, Stet, Studio, The Courier Mail, The Newcastle Herald, The Sydney Morning Herald, The Washing Machine, Verandah, Verso, Wastelands,* The New Zealand Poetry Society Anthology 1996, BGS Anthology 1991–1995, Five Dollar Freedom Essential Poetry Anthology, Harold Kesteven Poetry Prize Anthology 1991, IGGS Anthology, Seven Dollar Heaven Essential Poetry Anthology 1994, The Creativity Centre Anthology. Some have been broadcast by ABC Radio National in *A First Hearing*, Radio 5UV and Radio 2SER-FM.

This collection of poems was highly commended in the 1995 Jessie Litchfield Award for Literature and shortlisted in the 1993 Vincent Buckley Poetry Prize. It was first published in this form in 1998. Awards and citations for individual poems: 'Edward Kelly' (1995 John Dunmore Lang Poetry Prize); 'Photographer' (1992 Denis Butler Memorial Poetry Award); 'Tied Together' (1995 Golden Wattle Literary Award – third prize; 'A Day To Paint' (1992 Denis Butler Memorial Poetry Award – highly commended); 'Fish of Joy Lap the Waters of Sight' (1996 NZ Poetry Society International Poetry Competition – commended); 'Writing' (1996 Apollo Poetry

Award – commended); 'Manchineel Tree' (1992 Red Earth Poetry Award – commended); 'Hospital Room After Death' (1991 Harold Kesteven Poetry Award – commended).

The author gratefully acknowledges Writer-in-Residencies at Mabel Park State High School (1996), Ormiston College (1994), Ipswich Girls Grammar School (1993), Moreton Bay College (1993), Emerald Writers Week (1992), Ferny Hills State School (1991), McDowall State School (1991) and Writers Camps at Brisbane Grammar School (1992–96) and Brisbane Girls Grammar School (1992).